MOVIEMAKERS' FILM CLUB

Be a
FILM EDITOR

POLISH the Performance

by
Alix Wood

PowerKiDS press

New York

Published in 2018 by Rosen Publishing
29 East 21st Street, New York, NY 10010

CATALOGING-IN-PUBLICATION DATA
Names: Wood, Alix.
Title: Be a film editor: polish the performance / Alix Wood.
Description: New York : PowerKids Press, 2018. | Series: Moviemakers' film club | Includes
index.
Identifiers: LCCN ISBN 9781538323748 (pbk.) | ISBN 9781508162667 (library bound) | ISBN
9781538323755 (6 pack)
Subjects: LCSH: Motion pictures--Editing.
Classification: LCC TR899.W64 2018 | DDC 778.5'35--dc23

Produced for Rosen Publishing by Alix Wood Books
Designed by Alix Wood
Editor: Eloise Macgregor
Editor for Rosen: Kerri O'Donnell
Series consultant: Cameron Browne

Photo credits: Cover, 1, 4 top, 7, 8, 9, 11 12 middle and bottom, 14 middle, 15, 16, 17,
19, 20, 21, 22, 23, 24, 25, 26, 27, 18 © Adobe Stock Images; 4 bottom © Dreamstime; 6
© 1000words/Dreamstime; 10 © Reuters/Russell Boyce; 12 top © Derek Jensen; 14 left ©
Hillebrand Steve/U.S. Fish and Wildlife Service; 14 right © Pexels

Printed in the United States of America
CPSIA compliance information: Batch # BW18PK: For further information contact
Rosen Publishing, New York, New York at 1-800-542-2595.

CONTENTS

INTRODUCING THE EDITOR!

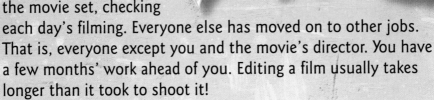

You have spent the last three months on the movie set, checking each day's filming. Everyone else has moved on to other jobs. That is, everyone except you and the movie's director. You have a few months' work ahead of you. Editing a film usually takes longer than it took to shoot it!

Most of an editor's work is done in **post-production**. Post-production is the period after the movie has been shot. The editor, with the director, makes decisions about what to keep in the movie, and what to cut out. During the edit, editors will work with the sound and visual effects departments. They add any music, sound, or graphics the movie may need.

Editing is done on a computer, using specialist computer **software**. There are editing **apps** that you can use on your smartphone, too, such as iMovie or PowerDirector.

A Film Editor Needs to...

- understand post-production
- be familiar with computer editing equipment
- understand a story's rhythm, pace, and tension
- be creative under pressure
- have excellent communication and people skills
- have technical knowledge
- understand what will look good on film
- be able to lead a team
- be patient
- pay attention to detail
- have good organizational skills
- work long hours

Cell Phone Movie School

Editors have to make the tough decisions, such as cutting some of the film to make a better movie. Sometimes, on a smartphone movie, the same person might write the script, direct the shoot, operate the camera, and edit the movie. In a perfect world, a different person should edit. A director or camera operator would find it very hard to cut a scene that they put so much effort into, even if it didn't really work.

"The film is made in the editing room. The shooting of the film is about shopping... you've got to make sure before you leave the store that you got all the ingredients. And then you take those ingredients and you can make a good cake - or not."

Philip Seymour Hoffman

STARTING THE EDIT

Editors are involved throughout the filming of a movie. First, they will read through the script to understand the **storyline**. Often scenes are shot out of sequence. The editor has to have a very clear idea of the story, to check each scene will flow well into the next when they are edited back into the right order. During filming, the editor or an assistant will check the day's tapes. They are looking for any errors that might affect their edit.

Checking The Day's Footage

Dailies, also known as rushes, are the raw footage from each day's shooting. Watching the dailies allows the editor and director to see how the filming is progressing. If anything needs to be reshot, it can be done straight away. Usually on a big-budget movie, all the main members of the crew will watch the dailies.

Editors might create a DVD for the director to take and watch at the end of the day's shoot.

Each department watches the dailies to check their own work. The camera crew checks that everything was shot correctly, and the sound crew checks the sound. Costume and makeup people check the clothes and hair.

The director, producer, and editor look at the movie as a whole. The director will tell the editor which parts they like best. Editors must note any problems spotted by each different crew. Some things are difficult to see on a small screen, so this opportunity to watch the day's filming on a big screen is important. When the screening is over, the editor will go back to the editing room with their notes and get to work.

The Editing Stages

Editors create their **editor's cut** from the dailies. There are several stages of movie editing. The editor's cut, sometimes called the assembly edit or rough cut, is the first stage. It is usually longer than the final film will be, and will be cut more at the next stage. The next edit is called the **director's cut**, which is then refined further to make the **final cut**.

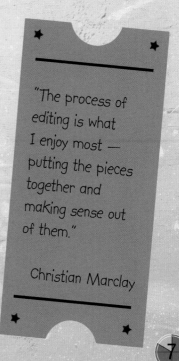

"The process of editing is what I enjoy most — putting the pieces together and making sense out of them."

Christian Marclay

CREATING STORIES

The screenwriter first creates the movie's storyline. The director and **director of photography** then take the story and bring it to life on set. Once the movie gets into the hands of the editor, you might think that the story just needs the finishing touches. Actually, the editor still has a huge influence on telling the story, too

Editing is like a puzzle, except there is no picture on the box lid to help you. You also have no idea how many pieces of the puzzle you need to use, or in what order! How would you order these clips?

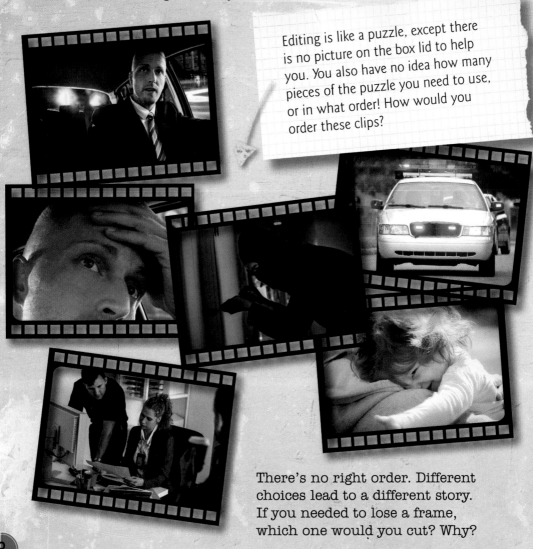

There's no right order. Different choices lead to a different story. If you needed to lose a frame, which one would you cut? Why?

Once the filming is complete, the editor's work on the story really begins. Every movie has what is know as a **story arc** — the story begins, the anticipation builds, then there is a **climax** where the film turns a corner around the middle of the story, then the action leads to the story's end. Each scene also has its own small story arc. Every important character has their own arc, too. The editor must keep track of all these arcs and piece them together.

Organizing and editing old rolls of film used to be a headache. Editing is much easier now. Smartphone apps or computer programs make sorting through hours of footage much easier.

Cell Phone Movie School

To keep track of a storyline, many editors pin notes on a wall to make a big **storyboard**. This helps them make sure they reveal things to the audience in the right order. When you edit, keep in mind that the **dialogue** in the clips must make sense, the story arc needs to make sense, and each character's journey must make sense. You don't want the clip of the guard dog looking vicious before the part where he sees the villain breaking in. That dog has a story arc, too!

SETTING THE PACE

An editor sets the pace of a movie by selecting the length of each shot, and whether to use action shots or still ones. Action scenes in movies usually have a very fast pace, quickly cutting from one shot to another. A romantic or sad scene is usually slow-paced. A slow pace gives the audience time to think, and feel emotionally connected to the story.

By controlling the pace, editors can control how the audience feels. A fast pace is exciting and gets the heart pumping. A slow pace allows the audience time to soak up the scene. If it is slow for too long, though, the audience may get bored. If it is too fast-paced for long periods, the audience might get worn out. Editors must learn when and why to change the pace.

Cell Phone Movie School

Comedies are mostly fast-paced, although not as fast as an action movie. Whenever a character is talking, they will be in the frame. Cuts are made at the end of each character's dialogue. This is known as "popcorn cutting." As the dialogue is usually snappy, so are the cuts.

Cuts on TV sitcoms such as *Friends* are usually fast-paced.

Normal pace is between a fast and a slow pace. Each shot usually lasts around 5 seconds. A normal pace is good for scenes showing everyday life. Most of a movie will be at a normal pace.

Editors have their own style of pace. If you gave the same footage to three different editors, you would get three different movies.

Mixing Up The Pace

A slow pace helps build up the tension in a scene. It allows the audience to anticipate what is going to happen next.

1. Our heroine is brushing her teeth in the bathroom (normal pace).
2. She hears a car on the driveway (slow pace—tension).
3. The door is kicked in, and two armed men run in (fast pace).
4. Heroine runs to find a place to hide (fast pace).
5. Heroine cowers in wardrobe (slow pace—tension).

normal pace   slow pace   fast pace

KNOWING THE SHOTS

Do you know your **master shot** from your **close-up**? Editors must know all the camera shots and how to use them.

An Establishing Shot
A shot of the building or landscape where the action is set. They are usually at the beginning of a scene or movie, to establish where the characters are.

A Master Shot
A master shot films a scene from beginning to end, and shows all the actors at once. The camera usually keeps still. The editor cuts other shots into the master shot, to mix up the pace, but will cut back to the master shot to show any movement.

A Sequence Shot
The camera moves with the actors, who are usually filmed from the front as they walk. The camera can be handheld, or pushed on a platform known as a dolly, along a track.

Sequence shots are great for showing busy places and changing scenery.

Playing With Distances and Angles

The director of photography will usually have taken shots from some different camera angles or distances in each scene. These shots are then used by the editor to break up the master shot and make the scene more interesting.

Close-up	Medium Shot	Long Shot	High Angle	Low Angle
Showing head and shoulders	Showing from the waist up	Showing the whole body	Shot from above	Shot from below

Cell Phone Movie School

Next time you watch a movie, pay attention to the different types of shots. The movie director and director of photography would have chosen which camera shots or angles best tell the story. The editor then chooses how to piece them together for the final film. Close-ups are good to show facial expressions and emotion. Long shots are great to show the surroundings. Shooting from below makes a person look big and powerful, while shooting from above makes them look small and powerless.

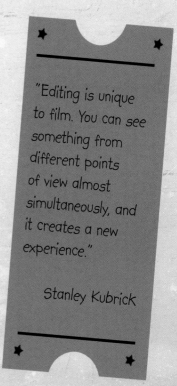

"Editing is unique to film. You can see something from different points of view almost simultaneously, and it creates a new experience."

Stanley Kubrick

MAKING CHOICES

The editor has to make the hard choices. They may have rolls and rolls of great footage, but they need to cut many hours of film into a one-and-a-half hour movie. Choosing what shots best tell the story is part of the editor's job.

The director of photography will often shoot extra footage for the edit, too, known as **B-roll**. B-roll is shot to help enrich the story. Imagine a scene with a father and son fishing at a lake. The main shots will be of the two characters, either both together, or in individual shots. The B-roll would be shots of the lake, of boats passing by, or close-ups of hands baiting the fishing rods. An editor will often insert B-roll to add interest, or help smooth the change between a long shot and close-up.

Long shot   B-roll insert   Close-up

Editors often use B-roll inserts in threes. This mimics a character moving their head from left to center to right as they take in the scenery around them.

Cell Phone Movie School

Cutting in a character's reaction to something can help make a scene more powerful. A character's response to events can be very important to the story. Try to film reaction shots to add into your final cut. You can include reaction shots from extras as well as the main characters.

Using Cutaways

A **cutaway** shows something related to the scene, but not part of the main action. For example, you could show a girl getting on the school bus, then a cutaway of the countryside through the bus window, then show the girl sitting in class. The cutaway bridges the gap between the two scenes and explains how the girl got from one place to the other without too many boring bus shots.

The edit makes a big difference to how an audience feels about a scene. Russian filmmaker, Lev Kuleshov, put an identical shot of an actor's face before an image of a bowl of soup and then a coffin. Audiences believed the actor's expression was different each time, but it was the same piece of film! The audiences' own emotions colored their view of the acting.

CUTTING

Once editors decide which shots they want to use, they have to decide how to cut the shots together. There are a lot of different ways to cut film.

Hard Cut

A **hard cut**, sometimes called a standard cut, simply cuts from one clip to another. Hard cuts are often used for phone conversations. If you want your audience to be in one moment, and then instantly in another, use a hard cut.

Jump Cut

If you want to cut from one frame to a later one from the same clip, use a **jump cut**. These cuts are a great, quick way to show passing time.

Quick jump cuts show this girl has waited a long time, without wasting the audience's time.

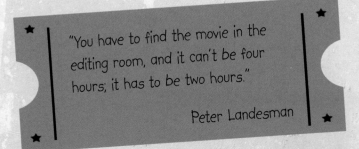

"You have to find the movie in the editing room, and it can't be four hours; it has to be two hours."

Peter Landesman

Cell Phone Movie School

Ever wondered why so many movies are filmed in low light? It may be because it helps editors make **invisible cuts**. An invisible cut fools the viewer into thinking the scene is one continuous take. To make an invisible cut, fill the end of one frame with something of a similar color to the beginning of the next. Perhaps you could pan the camera to film two actors typing in a dimly lit room. A dark frame between the shots would make it appear as if you filmed them continuously, even if the filming was done later. Try adding some invisible cuts to your movie.

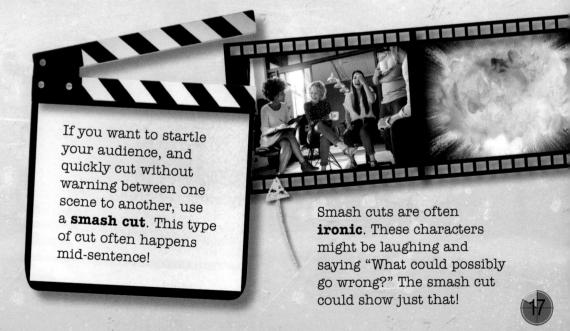

If you want to startle your audience, and quickly cut without warning between one scene to another, use a **smash cut**. This type of cut often happens mid-sentence!

Smash cuts are often **ironic**. These characters might be laughing and saying "What could possibly go wrong?" The smash cut could show just that!

17

L-CUTS AND J-CUTS

Cuts to the sound and picture don't always happen at the same time. Sometimes the sound overlaps a cut to the next picture, or the picture might overlap a cut to the next soundtrack. These cuts mimic real life. We may hear someone talking, and then turn our head to see them. Or while someone is talking, we may look at another person to see their reaction.

L-cuts

In an L-cut, you see the **video**, or picture, before you hear the soundtrack. For example, when Tom and Sarah are having a conversation, Tom is talking, but you see Sarah for a while before she starts talking.

J-cuts

In a J-cut, you hear the **audio**, or sound, before you see the picture that matches that audio. For example, Tom and Sarah are having a conversation. Sarah is talking, but the camera stays on Tom for a little while before you see Sarah.

They are called J-cuts and L-cuts because of the shape the cuts made in reels of film. The shape can still be seen in new editing software, where the audio runs under the video.

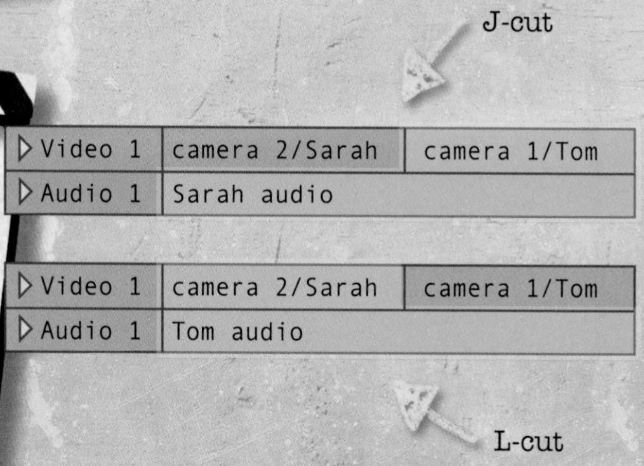

J-cut

▷ Video 1	camera 2/Sarah	camera 1/Tom
▷ Audio 1	Sarah audio	

▷ Video 1	camera 2/Sarah	camera 1/Tom
▷ Audio 1	Tom audio	

L-cut

L-cuts and J-cuts are mainly used during conversations. They help stop the cuts from one person to the other becoming too repetitive. Editor's can cut to the expression on the face of the nonspeaking actor. Even just showing an expressionless actor helps remind the viewer that this is a conversation between two people, and not just one person speaking in isolation.

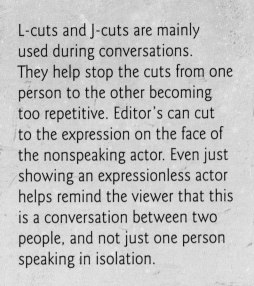

Cell Phone Movie School

Have fun playing with J-cuts and L-cuts, so you don't always show the obvious in your movie edit. J-cuts and L-cuts can be used with sound effects, too. It is more interesting to see a character's reaction to the noise of a train arriving than to just see footage of the train arriving.

Seeing a character's reaction makes a conversation seem more real.

19

CUTTING ON ACTION

The best cuts are ones that you don't notice. Cutting on action is a clever technique that editors use to disguise a cut. The editor makes a cut while there is some movement happening on screen. The viewer's eyes are drawn to the movement, and this takes their attention away from the cut itself.

Imagine you have a shot of a man putting a suitcase down on the ground. If you cut to a close-up of the suitcase as it hits the floor, in the middle of the movement, the cut will look seamless. It doesn't matter if the movement is fast, slow, big, or small. The same technique works just as well with a fast movement, such as the baseball game below.

The ball leaves the pitcher's hand and then draws the viewer into the shot of the batter.

Timing the cut is an art. You want to be able to see the ball leave the pitcher's hand, so the viewer follows its journey.

Cell Phone Movie School

Editors can only play with the footage that they are given. This is one of the reasons why it is useful for an editor to check the day's filming. They can advise the crew about any set-ups that may help a scene make the cut! For example, it is a good idea to let the actors know that if they make even a small head movement at the beginning and end of every take, you are more likely to be able to use it!

Editors tend to make a cut in the first third of the action. If someone is turning their head in a long shot, the start of the head turn will be in that shot, and then the final two-thirds will be in the close-up. When you watch movies and television, try to see when a cut on action is made. Does it always follow that rule?

Editors also need to match the action. All moving things need to be in the same place at the end of one cut and the beginning of the next shot.

TRANSITIONS

When editors have to connect shots that don't have much to link them, they may use **transitions**. Transitions are effects that bridge the join where one shot ends and another begins.

The Dissolve

In a **dissolve** transition, one clip **fades** into the next. It can be so subtle the viewer may not even be aware it is happening. The dissolve is most often used when there is a change in time, or **location**. It can also be used when there is a emotional link between two images.

Transitions work best if the two shots are similar to each other. The same horizon in this dissolve makes the transition seamless.

The Fade

A "fade out" is when the picture gradually turns to a single color, usually black or white. A "fade in" is when the picture gradually appears on screen. Fade ins are used at the beginning of a scene, and fade outs at the end of a scene.

You can use a dissolve as a **visual effect**. You might dissolve a boy's face over an old man's face, as if he is aging.

The Wipe

A **wipe** is where one shot replaces another either by an edge traveling from one side of the frame to another, or by using a shape.

A line wipe sweeps across the screen in any direction.

An iris wipe uses a growing or shrinking circle to wipe the screen.

A clock wipe sweeps the screen as the hands of a clock.

"Every aspect of filmmaking requires choice. The selection of the subject, the shooting, editing, and length are all aspects of choice."

Frederick Wiseman

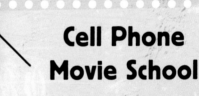

Cell Phone Movie School

Once you have decided what kind of transition will work best, you need to choose the best shots to place on either side of the transition. Try out all the shots you have, and then start to narrow down the ones that work well with each other. Look for similarities in the shots' colors, movement, or shapes, until you find a pair that works perfectly.

EDITING SOUND

On a big-budget movie, the final soundtrack would be produced by the sound editor. The editor would provide the sound editor with a **picture lock** edit. This edit is the final version of the movie for the images. The picture lock just needs the soundtrack to make it the final cut.

Spotting the Movie

Most sound is added during post-production. The editor, along with the director, goes through the movie, scene by scene, with the sound editor. They create a list of every sound that needs adding, tweaking, or replacing.

Dialogue is usually recorded during filming, but often needs fine-tuning later. Sometimes, actors will come back to the studio and re-record all the dialogue on a separate soundtrack.

Often composers create music specially for a movie. Music can be bought for use in a movie by the creators of the track. It is important to make sure you have permission to use all music and sound effects in your movie. Usually you must pay a fee to whoever owns the rights.

Everyday sounds are created by specialists known as **Foley artists**. They recreate sounds such as footsteps or doors slamming. You can also buy prerecorded sound effects from sound libraries.

Cell Phone Movie School

On a low-budget movie, editing the soundtrack might be a job that falls to the editor. There are several free sound editing programs you can download that will help you create great soundtracks on a smartphone. Each program works slightly differently, so watch some video tutorials to learn how yours works, and then experiment on your soundtrack.

Playing with the sound in your edit can help add to the characters in your story. You can make a bad guy louder, or slow down a lazy character's speech. Play with the settings and see what sounds right.

"By manipulating what you hear and how you hear it and what other things you don't hear, you can not only help tell the story, you can help the audience get into the mind of the character."

Walter Murch

ADDING EFFECTS

In post-production, movies are given their finishing touches. Any effects are added, and the editor will usually do some **color correction** and **color grading**.

Color grading is when editors give footage a color "look." Color grading can turn day into night, or make a washed-out piece of film bright and colorful. Color grading can alter the mood of a piece of film. A lighthearted movie could be colored to be bright, while a movie about a prison could be colored with cold grays and blues.

Editors color correct film to make the color consistent. The goal is to make every shot look as it would in real life. Footage from different cameras and lighting conditions can have very different results.

Adding color grading to a movie helps to give it atmosphere.

Special Effects

In a Hollywood movie, a visual effects team would create effects. For smaller budgets, the editor might create some simple effects. Editing software usually has filters and overlays that editors can use. For instance you can us motion effects, to make a movie look as if it was filmed using a handheld camera. Editors use prerecorded clips of effects such as explosions. These can be bought from film stock libraries and cut into a scene.

If your film crew forgot to blow fake snow at the actors, add some snow effects from an effects library.

Understanding color will help you when you edit it. Film uses the primary colors of red, green, and blue (RGB). Other colors are made by mixing these three colors. White is made by a mix of all three colors at full strength, and black is created when there are no colors.

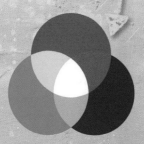

Cell Phone Movie School

Editing programs help you color grade and add visual effects. DaVinci Resolve, iMovie, Filmora, Hit Film Express, and Lightworks are either free or offer free trials. You can use a free trial to experiment with different looks and effects. If you want to upload your edited video, you may have to buy a license. Have a look online for tips and hints on how to use the different software.

GETTING YOUR EDIT SEEN

Once you have edited your movie, you will want people to watch it. A big Hollywood producer might be looking for someone with your talents! The easiest way to get your movie seen is to upload it to a video-sharing website.

Sharing Your Movie

Probably the best known video-sharing site is YouTube. There is a version for young people, known as YouTube Kids. The most popular video-sharing site for filmmakers is Vimeo. Ask a parent or caregiver if it is OK for you to share your movie. They will have to help you set up an account. You have to be over 13 years old to have your own YouTube account.

Remember that once something has gone online, it is there forever. Be sure your movie is something you are happy to share with anyone.

Getting Viewers

Here are some tips to help you get the most viewers for your movie.

- Choose a great thumbnail. When you upload your movie you can choose the image that appears in the search results, known as a thumbnail. Choose an exciting picture, and put the movie title on it.

- Tag your movie. Tags are single words or short phrases that people might search for, such as "adventure movie" or "zombies." Think of as many tag words as you can that accurately describe your movie.

- Share your movie on your family's Facebook and Twitter. Get friends and family to subscribe to your channel.

Cell Phone Movie School

When you first upload your movie, just invite friends and family to see it. That way, you can test if it will be a success. Feedback can help you perfect your movie. You can allow people to leave comments about your movie, but don't take bad reviews to heart. If you like, you can turn off comments, or choose to approve them before they are seen.

Cast

Scott
Eva
Tom
Joe
Maria
Erkki
Mike
Frank

JOS BLEAU
MARIA IVANOVA
HANS MUSTER
OLA NORDMANN
ERIKA MUSTERMANN
MATTI MEIKÄLÄINEN
GIORGOS ELLINAS
FRED NURK

Directed by
Screenplay by
Produced by
Editor
Director of Photography

JOE PUBLIC
CHANSIU MING
HERR SCHMIDT
SANTERI VIINAMÄKI
JANEZ NOVAK

Editors often create the **credits** – the list of names of people involved in making the movie. Make sure you get your name on the credits!

GLOSSARY

apps Applications.

audio Recorded sound.

B-roll Extra footage filmed to enrich the story.

climax The point of highest dramatic interest.

close-up Film image taken at close range and showing the subject on a large scale.

color correction Altering a film's colors to make them consistent.

color grading Altering and enhancing the color of a movie.

credits A list of all the cast and crew involved in the production.

cutaway The interruption of film action by inserting a view of something else.

dailies Raw footage of the day's filming.

dialogue Conversation given in a written story or play.

director of photography The person who is in charge of filming for a movie.

director's cut A version of a film that reflects the director's original intentions.

dissolve A gradual transition from one image to another.

editor's cut A rough first edit of a movie.

establishing shot Usually the first shot of a new scene, to show where the action is taking place.

fade A transition to and from a blank image.

final cut The final version of a film.

Foley artists Specialists who reproduce everyday sound effects that are added to a movie.

hard cut The change from one scene to another without any transition.

invisible cut A transition that cannot be seen.

ironic The use of words that mean the opposite of what one intends.

jump cut An abrupt transition from one scene to another.

location Place away from a studio where a movie is shot.

long shot View of a scene shot from a considerable distance.

master shot Film of an entire scene, from start to finish, from an angle that keeps all the players in view.

medium shot Camera shot in which the subject is in the middle distance.

picture lock All changes to the film cut have been done and approved.

post-production Work done on a film or recording after filming or recording has taken place.

sequence shot A long take that lasts an entire scene.

smash cut One scene abruptly cuts to another.

software The programs and other operating information used by a computer.

story arc The main plot of an ongoing storyline.

storyboard A sequence of drawings, representing the shots planned for a film or television production.

storyline The plot of a movie.

transitions The process or a period of changing from one state or condition to another.

video A recording of moving visual images.

visual effect A special effect that is added to a film or video in post-production.

wipe One shot replaces another by traveling across the frame or with a special shape.

FOR MORE INFORMATION

Books

Blofield, Robert. *How to Make a Movie in 10 Easy Lessons: Learn How to Write, Direct, and Edit Your Own Film Without a Hollywood Budget (Super Skills)*, Lake Forest, CA: Walter Foster Jr, 2015.

Green, Julie. *Shooting Video to Make Learning Fun (Explorer Library: Information Explorer)*. North Mankato, MN: Cherry Lake Publishing, 2013.

Websites

Due to the changing nature of Internet links, PowerKids Press has developed an online list of websites related to the subject of this book. This site is updated regularly. Please use this link to access the list:

www.powerkidslinks.com/mm/editor

INDEX